AF481276

GROWING MINDS
BOOKS

# ANOTHER GREAT DAY

Dr. Isaiah Varisano

Today was
another great
day.

I had a
delicious
breakfast.

My family was
home all day.

I painted a new
picture.

My friends
came over to
visit.

We built a fort.

I learned a new song.

I played
outside.

# We had my favorite food for lunch.

I played dress
up.

I relaxed.

I took a good
nap.

I cuddled.

I laughed a lot.

I took a bath
with bubbles.

I used my new
toothbrush.

# I was read a bedtime story.

I was kissed
goodnight.

# Savoring the Positive

The negativity bias is a psychological phenomenon where humans tend to give more weight and attention to negative experiences or information compared to positive ones. To counter this tendency, it is important to consciously create a habit of noticing the good things. Actively noticing and savoring positive experiences contributes to a positive emotional state, enhancing mood and overall emotional well-being. Cultivating a habit of recognizing the good can contribute to greater resilience, helping individuals cope more effectively with life's challenges. Focusing on positive aspects fosters an optimistic outlook, influencing how individuals perceive and approach various situations in life.

# Benefits of Optimism

Hundreds of studies have been conducted on optimism correlating it with better...

- social support
- relationship satisfaction
- wellbeing and quality of life
- mental health
- immune response
- lifespan
- work, school, and athletic performance
- coping skills
- success
- job satisfaction/offers/promotions
- resilience

AND MORE!